What Happens at Horse Shows?

A beginner's guide for parents navigating the world of hunter jumper horse shows

Elizabeth Page

Dedicated to Miss Anita,

the person responsible for bringing me

into the horse world, and

to Ginger,

my mentor at the show ring.

Table of Contents

1 Introduction

This book is meant for parents just entering the horse show world. I took no knowledge for granted because I remember what it felt like to be brand new to the horse world when my daughter began riding at the age of seven.

For years I have been hoping for something that listed all the answers to questions that I didn't even know to ask. So, here's a synopsis of what I've learned over many years. There is still plenty that I don't know, but thankfully I have a very knowledgeable and patient daughter and trainer to guide me through the confusion. I also recommend befriending a knowledgeable mom who perhaps rode as a child. I'm lucky to know quite a few from our barn.

I don't pretend to have written an official guide to hunter jumper shows. These pages represent my impressions while experiencing shows in the southeastern U.S. I sincerely thank my daughter Bailey and her trainer, Catherine Tucker, for graciously reviewing the text and offering corrections and excellent suggestions. I'd also like to thank Becky Apple, who helped Bailey develop her strong riding skills to become the rider she is today and who patiently explained the horse world to me (over and over again). Finally, I thank my husband Dan for supporting Bailey's riding ambitions and my idea for turning our experiences into a book.

I refer you to the experts to learn more about the details of shows. The United States Equestrian Federation (USEF) has a wealth of information on their website (http://www.usef.org/), and you can also contact your local hunter jumper association.

This book is roughly organized in the order that activities occur during a weekend show. I've pulled out some of the information as reference guides and organized them in Section 7.

2 Before the show

Preparations begin well before the show. Here are a few reminders of things you'll want to do. Of course your child's trainer will help guide you through the process.

2.1 "A" shows versus "C" shows

Shows are classified based on the prize money that is awarded. "A" or "AA" shows award the most money, while "C" shows can take place without awarding prize money. There are also "B" shows, but I have never been to one. As you can imagine, the higher classified shows have higher expenses to attend them. You will pay more for class fees and stalls, but you child may win back some of his or her fees. "A" and "AA" shows also attract more experienced riders and fancier horses. From a parent's point of view, "A" shows are lavish. There are more vendors set up in fancy tents. Often there are evening activities that may include dinners, exhibitions or a mini-prix or a grand prix.

2.2 Paperwork

Before the show, you will want to send in your child's entry form. You should coordinate the classes in which your child will show with your trainer. Keep in mind you can always add or scratch classes once you arrive at the show. Both you and your child's trainer need to sign this form. If you are unable to register before the show, you can do so at the show grounds, but there may be an extra charge.

In some ways horse shows are like music recitals, you normally perform a piece that is easier than what you practice during lessons. With all the stress and distractions of the show, riders need to compete in classes in which they are competent, not the ones they are just learning. Makes sense, right? Ok, now explain that to an eight year old who is told to compete in Walk-Trot when she had been cantering in lessons. However, once you move up, you can't go back. One of my daughter's friends once said wistfully, when waiting for Walk-Trot-Canter to begin, "I miss Walk-Trot, you just walk, and you trot..."

Class sheets/prize lists contain the schedule of the show and can be found online and downloaded from the Website of the organization sponsoring the show. These sheets come in handy during the show to help monitor the progress of the divisions and classes, so you might want to keep one in your pocket. Updated versions are available in the office during the show.

2.3 What to take

Your trainer will make sure that the horse arrives at the show. He or she may also transport the tack and tack trunks from the barn. You will be responsible for getting your rider there, and making sure your child has show clothes, a helmet and anything else that you may have taken home to launder (girth, saddle pads, etc.).

2.3.1 Tack trunk list

Do you need a tack trunk? Tack trunks can come in very handy because everything you need for the show can be loaded in it. They are sturdy and portable. However, a large plastic tub can also be used and is much less expensive. If your child decides to commit to this sport, you may want to consider investing in a sturdy tack trunk, but there is no reason you can't wait awhile to make sure this isn't a short-term sport. See Section 7 for a list of items to have in your tack trunk based on a list our trainer developed.

A tack trunk will hold all of the essentials needed for a show.

2.3.2 Car loading checklist

If you are traveling a long distance to the show, you want to make sure you have everything in the car. Although there are usually tack stores with mobile units at the show, it is so much nicer to just remember everything instead. At the very least, make sure really expensive things like the show helmet, pants, and jacket are in there. I've shared a checklist in Section 7, which we keep in the car.

2.4 Items of convenience/comfort

2.4.1 Bikes

Bikes come in handy at horse shows. Although when you first arrive, everything might seem like a short walk away. However, as the weekend goes on, those short walks seem to lengthen. Having a bike or two at the show allows you to take a quick trip from the barn up to the ring to check on how the schedule is progressing.

2.4.2 Collapsible chairs

Camping chairs are good for venues that don't have bleachers at the rings. Also, it can be nice to have a place to sit back at the barn with the other parents after the show while your kids clean their tack and take care of their horses.

2.4.3 Cooler/snacks

Having cold drinks and snacks at the show ring is very important. As you can imagine, sitting in the sun on a horse in a wool jacket can become extremely uncomfortable. On really hot days, the judges may make jackets optional. Regardless, a cold drink can help keep your child from becoming over-heated. Also, if your child is too nervous to eat in the morning, having a snack at the ring will be great for when he or she is suddenly hungry and the snack stand line is too long to wait in. So, bring a cooler that you can leave in your car or at the barn, and bring a smaller, portable cooler that can be kept on your trainer's golf cart or at the show ring.

2.4.4 Rain Gear

Don't forget your rain jacket (with a hood!) Horse shows will go on even in the pouring rain. Bring a jacket for yourself and your child. You can spend a lot of time standing in the rain. Also, some type of waterproof blanket can be nice to keep all of that expensive leather tack a little drier. Even if the show takes place in a covered ring, your child may be waiting outside in the rain. After un-tacking the horse, make sure your child cleans his or her saddle well to prevent water staining.

2.5 Arriving at the show

Once you find where your barn is located at the stables and have helped unpack and set up, you will need to check in with the show office.

Communication with your trainer is very important. Especially when you are new to the sport and just learning how things work. I've caught myself getting into circular conversations because I didn't even realize what I was trying to ask. For instance, we leased a pony from a good friend just for a show, and he arrived at the show without shoes. One of my knowledgeable mom friends was concerned because a horse without shoes can injure a hoof or leg by stepping on a rock or something else at the show grounds. So, I asked our trainer if it was a problem that the pony didn't have shoes, and she said that she had pulled them off because he moves better without them. I was confused because I knew he normally wore shoes, and I didn't understand how he could move better if we had to worry about where he was stepping. She then explained that without the weight of the shoes on his feet, he could lift them farther off the ground, which looks better in the show ring. Light bulb! Now I understood that the shoes were supposed to be off to help the pony perform better at the show. However, we took the precaution of wrapping his feet in diapers and duct tape for traveling to the ring.

2.5.1 Checking in

When you arrive at the show, you need to check in at the show office and pick up your child's number. If you did not register ahead of time, you will need to specify the classes in which your child will compete and leave a check. Your child's trainer can help you select the appropriate classes. I take a class sheet and circle the class numbers as we discuss the appropriate ones for my daughter.

Your child will wear a number tied around his or her waist while showing. You will find what looks like long shoestrings in the office to thread through the holes on each side of the number. It's best to loop the strings through twice because they tend to tear through during really warm shows when sweaty numbers become an issue.

Updated class sheets can also be found in the show office. If you haven't brought one with you, you might want to take one to help keep track of how the show is progressing. The office may also post how many people have entered in each class to give you a rough idea how long each division will take to complete.

2.5.2 Adding and scratching

If you and your trainer decide to add classes in which your child will compete, you'll need to fill out an add slip at the show office. You'll need your child's number and the class number to fill out the short form. You should also let the in-gate person know that your child will be riding in that event. The same holds true for scratching, or removing your child from a class.

3 Day of the Show

So, today is the day! Your trainer will let you know when you should arrive at the show grounds. If your child is riding later in the day, he or she may want to arrive in schooling clothes rather than show clothes. If he or she is riding early, show clothes should be worn.

3.1 Show Clothes

Your child probably already owns a black helmet and a pair of paddock boots for lessons. Younger kids can wear those same boots for shows, although you might want to polish them before the show. The rest of the outfit includes jodhpurs (riding pants), a show shirt with a collar, jacket, and garters. It's always nice to find friends at the barn who have show clothes they have outgrown, and most tack stores have consignment sections with gently worn show clothes.

Younger riders wear paddock boots, jodhpurs and garters as part of the show wardrobe.

3.1.1   Tall boots

Sometime between 12 and 15 years of age your child's trainer will break the news to you – your child needs to start showing in tall boots. I remember when this happened to me. I had the fact in my head that kids don't wear tall boots until age 14. My daughter's trainer found this rule of thumb puzzling and quickly convinced me that my daughter was not going to be able to follow this arbitrary rule. Tall boots look really impressive, but more importantly, they help your child grip the saddle. The safety aspect was the one that convinced me to make the investment. They are pricey and difficult/painful to break in. So, finding used boots is great for the price and the fact someone else had done the hard part of breaking them in. Most tall boots now have zippers extending up the back, which make putting them on and more importantly taking them off much easier. Unfortunately, as we found out, zippers can break, which is very inconvenient at a show.

Older riders wear tall boots and breeches in shows.

3.1.2   Jodhpurs vs. Breeches

This brings us to the difference between jodhpurs and breeches. It took me a long time to figure out the differences between the two. Jodhpurs are worn with paddock boots. They have stirrups that slip over the boot and have cuffs at the bottom. Breeches are designed to be tucked into tall boots. They taper at the calf and close above the ankle with Velcro. Thin knee socks are worn over them, which are covered by the boots. So, if you have a young child who is not yet wearing tall boots, buy jodhpurs.

3.1.3   Braids and Ribbons

What about hair? Well, for boys it's easy, just put on your helmet and go. Girls have a few more options. They can pull it back in a hairnet so that it is hidden under the helmet, or younger girls can wear braids tied in ribbons. Nothing is more adorable than a little girl cantering by with her braids and ribbons bouncing along with her.

Braids and ribbons are adorable on younger riders, while older riders tuck their hair in their helmet with the help of a hairnet.

3.2   Tacking up

One of the many great things about horse shows is the responsibility your child takes on. At some point you may hear "we need to get my horse tacked up, can you bring me my bridle?" Yikes! What in the world is a bridle? Well, here's a quick tutorial on what the horse "wears" in the show ring.

The saddle goes on first, which means the saddle pad and then the saddle. The girth is the thick strap with buckles on each end that attaches the saddle to the horse. It goes on next and is fastened loosely at first and then tightened right before the rider mounts.

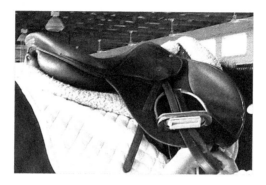

Your rider will put the saddle on first.

The bridle goes on last and fits over the horse's head and is attached to the bit, which goes in the horse's mouth and the reins, which are held by your child. The throat latch of the bridle is tightened so that you have a hand's width between the horse's cheek and the strap. The noseband is tightened under the chin snuggly. If a martingale is used, it goes on before the bridle and while you are attaching the girth.

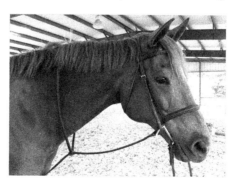

The bridle helps your rider steer the horse. A martingale can be used in over fences classes.

3.2.1 What's the purpose of a martingale?

A martingale goes over the horse's head and rests on his or her neck and attaches to the bridle and the girth. It is used in jumping classes to help keep the horse's head down. It is not used in flat classes because the rider is supposed to keep the horse's head down without the help of a martingale. So, if your child is using a martingale in jumping classes, make sure it comes off before he or she goes back in the ring for the flat classes.

3.3 Leading a horse

When leading a horse, you stand with the horse on your right. The horse should let you lead. If the horse starts to walk in front of you, make a small circle and then continue forward.

The horse should follow your lead.

3.4 Schooling

Prior to entering the show ring, your child will work with his or her trainer to practice riding and jumping. Depending on the trainer, he or she may want your child at the show before it begins to practice in the ring where your child will ride. Usually this is done for jumping classes so that the horse can see all the jumps ahead of time to reduce the chance of being spooked by a particularly scary looking flower or shrub.

Just prior to your child going into the ring, his or her trainer will want to go to the schooling ring to warm up the horse. The schooling ring often has many riders and trainers in it at the same time, going different directions. To me, this is the scariest place at the show. If you get nervous, it may be a good time to check out the snack stand, or chat with your fellow horse show parents.

4   In the show ring

4.1   What to take to the show ring

Since one of your many roles at the show will be to serve as your rider's "pit crew," I've included this checklist of items that captures what I have found handy to have at the show ring to keep your horse and rider show-ready. A version without the explanations of each item appears in Section 7.

— Water for drinking
— Hoof dressing for giving the horse's toes a shiny look
— Fly spray for pesky pests
— Towel (hand towel) for wiping down anything and everything
— Collar & pin (hopefully your child is already wearing them)
— Gloves (hopefully your child is already wearing them)
— Pen for writing on ribbons
— Tail brush for any last minute shavings stuck in the tail
— Grooming brush for cleaning the horse's legs after schooling
— Horse treats to thank the horse
— Snack for your child who may be waiting a long time
— Hoof pick for scraping off hooves after schooling and before applying hoof dressing
— Spray gel for mane (human gel works for unruly horse hair)
— Scissors for stray threads and unforeseen crises
— Safety pins for lost buttons, torn numbers, etc.
— Bobbie pins for last minute hair adjustments
— Spurs for pokey ponies/horses
— Crop for pokey ponies/horses
— Sunscreen for your rider and you

— Camera/video camera to capture the event

Bring your tack box or show bag to the show ring with all of your necessities.

4.2 Divisions and Classes

What is the difference between a division and a class? What are all these cryptic divisions? Why are teenagers riding in the Children's division? And, what exactly is a Pre-child?

Divisions are groups of classes. Each class (e.g., Walk-Trot Under Saddle) has a separate number. Once you know the division in which your rider will compete, you can determine which classes to follow.

4.2.1 Beginning divisions

When young kids start showing, they usually start with Walk-Trot. It sounds easy, but they learn quite a bit in these classes that they will carry with them to more advanced divisions. They have a chance to ride with many other horses in the ring and learn to spread out so that they have their own place on the rail (the fence around the ring) while trying to go by the judge as often as possible.

From Walk-Trot, they move up to Walk-Trot-Canter, and then to Crossrails when they begin to jump. This category can have different names (Beginning Rider or Young Entry). Crossrails are 18 inches high, and the courses can be as simple as going twice around the ring in a circle/oval with four jumps on the rail.

4.2.2 Flat Classes

Beyond Walk-Trot, all flat classes, meaning those not involving jumping, will include some combination of walk, trot, and canter. Most divisions have a flat class associated with them, so be aware of when those are scheduled because your child will need to be in the ring even if his or her place in the jumping lineup is scheduled for later.

A flat class

4.2.3 Over fences (Jumping) Classes

Divisions that include jumping classes can also be based on the age of the rider. The show season goes from December 1 to November 30 of the next year, so your horse show age is the one you have on December 1. Divisions such as 11 and under, 12-14, and 15-17 all refer to the age of the rider. There is also an age limit on Short Stirrup of 12 years. However, there is a similar division called Long Stirrup for riders older than 12. As the age range goes up, so does the height of the jumps in that division.

The Children's division refers to riders under the age of 18. There is a corresponding Adult division appropriately named for riders over 18. The Pre-Children's division has shorter jumps and is meant for riders working up to the Children's division.

Jumping classes span a wide range of ages and abilities.

The riders in jumping classes are often broken into smaller groups or "rotations." Each rider in the rotation trades off until they have ridden all the jumping classes in the division. Your trainer may ask you to place your rider in a specific rotation with the in-gate person to help avoid trainer conflicts.

4.2.4 Pony divisions

Ponies are classified as horses that are less than 14.2 hands. Horses are measured in hands from their withers to the ground, where one hand is equal to four inches. In describing a horse's height, the 14 refers to the number of whole hands, while the 0.2 refers to the number of inches remaining in its height. So a pony is less than 58 inches tall. Ponies are also further divided into size categories, small, medium, and large. A pony is considered small if it is 12.2 hands (50 inches) tall or shorter. Medium ponies are taller than 12.2 hands but no taller than 13.2 hands (54 inches). Therefore, large ponies are taller than 13.2 hands, but no taller than 14.2 hands. You may hear someone say that an owner has a "pony card." That means the pony has been officially measured and the owner has documentation certifying the height of the pony.

The division "Ponies" sets the height of the jump based on the size of the pony. In "C" shows small ponies usually jump 2ft 3in, mediums 2ft 6in, and larges 2ft 9in.

4.2.5 Jumper divisions

The Jumper divisions refer to a different type of riding. These divisions involve a time element. Jumpers are expected to ride through

14

complicated courses with tight turns without knocking the jump rails down within a certain time period. The rider wants a clean round, meaning no rails are knocked down and no jumps are refused within the time limit. Some classes include a jump off. The goal during the jump off is to move through a shorter course cleanly as fast as possible. The fastest rider wins. These classes are very exciting to watch and easy for the novice observer to follow.

4.2.6   Green divisions

These divisions are for green or inexperienced horses. Horses that have been showing for less than two years can show in these divisions. The point is to let them become more comfortable with the show experience.

4.2.7   Types of classes within a division

Divisions have different classes that are described by specific adjectives. These adjectives indicate how the class will be judged. Your rider will adjust what they concentrate on while in the ring based on these adjectives.

Equitation is judged on the rider. Equitation classes can include flat classes (no jumping with all the riders in the ring at the same time) and jumping classes. In flat classes the rider should have tight reins, be on the right lead while cantering and the correct diagonal while trotting, and sit up with a slightly arched back and shoulders back.

Under saddle is judged on the horse. The challenge to the rider is to make the horse look good, meaning move nicely.

Pleasure classes are in the Walk-Trot and Walk-Trot-Canter divisions. Loose reins are the key here, and the rider and the horse should be having fun, or at least look like they are having fun.

Hunter divisions include flat classes and jumping classes. These are judged on the horse, but the rider plays an important role in making sure that the horse goes smoothly around the course and "gets the numbers" meaning takes the intended number of strides between jumps and spreads them out evenly.

Medal jumping classes often have cash prizes and include unique tasks during the round. Riders may be asked to halt in the middle of the class and perhaps back up. They also might be required to trot a jump.

4.3 The workings of the show ring

The show will follow the schedule in the prize list. Your child will need to be tacked up and ready to go outside the ring well before he or she is due to go in. For flat classes, he or she will be in the ring with the other horses and riders competing in the class. For jumping classes, riders go in by themselves. Trying to figure out exactly when that will be is the greatest challenge of being a horse show parent.

How do you predict when your child will ride? To me the only thing more difficult than forecasting the weather is guessing when my daughter will be in the ring, especially if I'm trying to let my husband know when to be there to watch. Horse shows give new meaning to the phrase "hurry up and wait."

4.3.1 In-Gate Person

The in-gate person runs the show for that ring. He or she is a wealth of information and keeps track of when riders will go. Your trainer may ask you to post your child at a certain place in the lineup. You do this by talking to the in-gate person. To avoid conflicts with other riders from your barn, your trainer may want your child to go in the first group, or perhaps toward the end. The in-gate person is usually willing to work with you to help that ring run smoothly. Also, this person usually has the ribbons for each class sitting at the same table, and you can pick up your rider's ribbons from him or her.

4.3.2 What are trips?

A trip is one rider going through a jumping class. Depending on the division, there may be one to three trips for each rider. Often the announcer will say how many trips are left in a ring in a certain division. You can estimate how much time is left based on how long trips and transitions are taking. A rule of thumb is 2 minutes per trip, but they can move faster, so you need to stay on top of how the division is progressing.

4.4   Your role at the show ring

Beyond giving moral support, you can take on other tasks, similar to a pit crew. Armed with your tack box/show bag, you can make sure that your rider's boots are clean and jacket and number look good, hair is tucked neatly in the helmet, or ribbons are tied tightly. As for the horse, brush off his or her legs. Clean off any mud or other substances, and scrape off the hooves. Now is a good time to paint on hoof dressing. Paint an even, continuous line just below the coronet (the top of the hoof), and then fill in to the bottom edge. You can also make some finishing touches on the horse before your rider enters the ring by brushing out the tail or mane (the mane should lie on the horse's right). Make sure if your child is about to go into a flat class that the horse's martingale has been removed.

4.4.1   Clapping at the end of a trip

One helpful hint, make sure to watch your child's trainer for the cue on when to clap after a jumping round. Sometimes it's not obvious when it's over, and you really don't want to confuse your child when she or he is trying to remember the course. Yes, I have learned this from experience.

4.4.2   Being excused from the ring

If a rider falls off his or her horse, he or she will be excused from the ring. This means that class is over for him or her and he or she will not place in that class. Other reasons for dismissal include going off course (taking the jumps out of order), or the horse refusing a specific jump three times. Obviously, these situations can be very frustrating for your child, but include some of the tough lessons learned in the show ring.

4.5   Trainer conflicts

Trainer conflicts can occur when several riders from your barn are riding in different events at the same time. The people running the show will work around these conflicts with your trainer, but you also need to be proactive. Keep informed of how many trips away your child is from going into the ring. This is also a good way for your child to learn how to manage time. In my experience, a class will be held for trainer conflicts in jumping events, but not necessarily for flat classes.

You can make sure an experienced rider or parent is there from the barn to help out in the flat classes when your trainer is not available. I have found the exceptions to be Walk-Trot and Walk-Trot-Canter classes, which have been held until all the trainers arrived at the ring.

4.6 Judging

Each class is judged based on certain criteria. As you child becomes more experienced, expectations of his or her riding will grow.

4.6.1 Walk-Trot

The main things to think about are that the horses are spread out on the rail, the kids are on the right diagonal when they trot, and they trot when they are told to trot and walk when told to walk.

4.6.2 Walk-Trot-Canter

All the things in Walk-Trot still apply, plus the riders must pick up the correct lead in the canter.

4.6.3 Crossrails

Riders jump in this class. They need to start thinking about lead changes, memorizing the course, and getting the numbers.

4.6.4 Short/Long-Stirrup and other jumping classes

The courses become more complicated, and riders are expected to get the numbers, although they are allowed to add a stride without penalty. They also have to remember everything expected from riders in the lower divisions.

4.6.5 Jumpers

It's all about memorizing a complicated course, not knocking rails down, and doing so as fast as you can.

4.6.6 Getting the numbers

Some of the jumps in a course have an expected number of strides between them. These will be different for horses and ponies. When riders "gets the numbers", they take the correct number of strides between these jumps. Riders are said to "chip" when they take a short step right before jumping. In divisions like Crossrails and Short Stirrup, riders are allowed to add a stride.

4.7 Ribbons

Ribbons are "pinned" in each class. 1st through 6th place are awarded, so classes with 6 or fewer entries are my favorites because everyone goes home with a ribbon. The colors are blue for first place, red for second, yellow for third, white for fourth, pink for fifth, and green for sixth. It's a good idea to keep a pen with you at the show ring and write the details of the class on the back for later reference. You want to include your child's name, the horse's name, the division, the class, and the date it was awarded.

Ribbons Awarded

Place	Color	Points toward Champion
1st	Blue	10
2nd	Red	6
3rd	Yellow	4
4th	White	2
5th	Pink	1
6th	Green	$\frac{1}{2}$

What do you do with these ribbons? They can tend to pile up. My daughter hung hers in a border just below her ceiling, which then became rows of ribbons across her wall. One of her friends hung a net on the wall, which she used as a ribbon hanger. Others have made shadow boxes of ribbons and favorite photos and even quilts; the possibilities are endless.

4.7.1 Champion/Reserve Champion

For each division, which is a series of classes, a winner (Champion) and a runner-up (Reserve Champion) are declared. Points are assigned based on the ribbons awarded for each class. First place is worth 10 points, second place 6 points, third place 4 points, fourth place 2 points, fifth place 1 point, and sixth place ½ point. The champion of the division has the highest number of points when all of his or her ribbons are counted for each class in the division. The champion ribbon is larger than the ribbons awarded in the individual classes and combines blue, red and yellow ribbons. The reserve champion is the person with the next highest amount of points. This person receives a large ribbon that is made up of red, yellow and white ribbons. Ties are normally broken by reviewing who placed higher in the over fences (jumping) classes. Some shows only give champion ribbons for the weekend while others award champion each day of the show.

Points accumulate over the show year in each category and a year-end champion ribbon is awarded to the person with the most points. Of course the number of points accumulated depends both on the ribbons your rider receives and the number of shows you attend. Don't get me wrong, these year-end ribbons are really impressive, but be careful about getting caught up in point chasing. Your rider may find showing is more fun if he or she moves up divisions when ready rather than just at the beginning of show season. Doing this will distribute points over more than one division and affect year-end totals. Which approach your rider takes is a decision for you, your child, and your trainer to make together.

5 After the Show

You've made it through the weekend and are almost ready to go home. Here are the details of wrapping everything up.

5.1   Checking out

After your child has completed all the classes for the show, you need to go back to the show office to check out. If you forget, don't worry; they have your check from when you checked in. The person working in the office will print out an invoice for you with all of your charges including class fees, stalls, shavings, etc. Look it over and make sure everything looks ok, meaning your child really competed in all the classes listed, and you aren't being charged for five stalls when you only brought one horse. I haven't run into many mistakes, but they can happen. A special bonus on your invoice is that it will include how your child placed in each class (in case you forgot to write the class on the ribbons as you were collecting them).

5.2   Packing up

After the show, all that's left to do is pack everything up and head home. Your trainer will let you know what your role in helping out should be. At the very least, you should make sure your child's tack box is packed, and all the tack is clean and ready to be loaded. Make one last pass through the barn to make sure you didn't leave anything behind.

5.3   Heading home

Congratulations, you made it through the show! It's time to head home with your weary, but hopefully happy child.

6   Glossary

Bay – is a darker brown color of a horse or pony.

Bit – is a piece of tack that attaches to the bridle and goes into the horse's mouth. Bits are designed to make the horse respond to pulling on the reins.

Breeches – are pants designed to be tucked into tall boots. They taper at the calf and close above the ankle with Velcro. Thin knee socks are worn over them, which are covered by the boots.

Bridle – is the piece of tack that is put over the horse's head and is attached to the reins and the bit, which goes into the horse's mouth.

Buckskin – is a color of horse that corresponds to that of buckskin, sort of a light tan color.

Champion – of a division has the highest number of points based on the ribbons received for each class. The champion ribbon is larger than the ribbons awarded in the individual classes and combines blue, red and yellow ribbons.

Chestnut – is a reddish-brown color of horse or pony.

Chipping – occurs when a horse needs to take a short stride right before going over a jump.

Class – is an individual event at the show.

Class sheet – is the schedule of the show. This is also part of the prize list.

Diagonal – is the orientation of the rider during a posting trot with respect to the horse's leg. The rider should be going up when the horse's outside front leg (that toward the fence) is going forward.

Division – is a series of classes that are grouped together (for instance, Walk-Trot). Champion and Reserve Champion are pinned for a division.

Drag – during the show, a tractor will come into the ring and "drag" it to smooth the sand out. No horses are allowed in the ring with the tractor. This process is similar to a Zamboni in an ice skating rink, and the sand in the ring will look smooth and even after it has been dragged.

Equitation – refers to the action of the rider. Equitation classes are judged on the performance of the rider.

Fence – is a jump in the show ring.

Flat class – means that horses do not jump as part of the class. It can include walking, trotting and cantering and is also referred to as a hack.

Flying lead change – is a lead change that occurs while the horse is cantering.

Garters – are long strips of leather with buckles that wrap around the leg of younger riders who wear paddock boots in the show ring. They are worn to help riders grip the saddle better with their legs.

Getting the numbers – means a rider successfully makes the required number of strides between jumps.

Girth – is the long strap that goes around the horse's belly and attaches to the saddle. A fuzzy girth has fleece on the side that goes against the horse's belly.

Hack – this term means to ride your horse in the ring without jumping. A hack can include walking, trotting and cantering. In the context of a horse show, it means a flat class where all the riders in the class are in the ring riding at the same time.

Half chaps – are leather and are worn over the calf of the rider and extend from the top of the paddock boot to just below the knee. They act as a tall boot would and help the rider grip the saddle better. These are worn to school the horse, not in the show ring.

Half pad – is a small saddle pad that helps the saddle fit the horse better and provides more cushion between the saddle and the horse.

Halter – is the piece of tack that is basically a bridle without a bit. It goes around the horse's head. The lead rope is attached to it and it is used for transporting horses from the stable to the pasture, or anywhere else you might want to take them.

Helmet – is protective headgear. Most shows require that the helmet worn in the ring meet ASTM/SEI requirements. The American Society for Testing Material/Safety Equipment Institute set standards for equestrian use. When you purchase your helmet, there should be a tag on it saying that it meets these standards.

Hoof dressing – is a liquid that is brushed on the front of a horse's hooves before it goes into the ring (kind of like nail polish). His or her hooves are left looking clean and shiny like after a pedicure.

Horse show age – is the age your child was on December 1st of the previous year.

In-gate person – works the show ring and keeps track of the lineup of entries in the division and manages the riders going into the ring. This person usually has the ribbons for each class sitting nearby.

Irons – is another name for stirrups. Riders may be asked to "drop their irons" in a flat class, which means to take their feet out of their stirrups.

Jodhpurs – are pants worn with paddock boots by younger riders at shows. They have stirrups that slip over the boot and cuffs at the bottom.

Jog – is done in some divisions to allow the judge to evaluate the soundness of the horse. The rider dismounts from the horse, and then runs alongside as the horse trots in front of the judge.

Knocking a fence – means that the pole on the jump is knocked down during a jumping round.

Lead – refers to the leg that is leading when the horse is cantering. The horse's inside front leg should land after the outside front leg during the canter. Judges count off for riders who are on the wrong lead.

Lead change – refers to when the horse changes the foot that is leading in the canter.

Lead line – is a class where riders are led around the ring on their horses by lead ropes. This class is for riders not quite ready for Walk-Trot.

Lead rope – is a rope for leading the horse that attaches to the halter.

Martingale – is a piece of tack made of leather that horses wear in jumping classes. It helps keep the horse's head down. It goes around the horse's neck and attaches to the girth and the nose band of the bridle.

On the flat – refers to classes that don't include jumping. All the horses competing in the class are in the ring at the same time.

Over fences – refers to jumping classes.

Oxer – is a wider jump that has two sets of rails spaced a short distance apart. It looks like two jumps pushed together.

Paddock boots – are short leather boots that extend over the ankle (like high top tennis shoes). They are normally worn for lessons and schooling at shows and by younger girls in the show ring.

Pleasure – refers to classes in the Walk-Trot and Walk-Trot-Canter divisions that are judged based on whether the rider and the horse are having fun, or at least look like they are having fun.

Posting trot – involves the rider moving up and down as the horse trots.

Prize list – refers to the booklet (usually available online) that contains all the information about a show. The prize list contains the entry form and the class sheet (schedule) for the show.

Rail – is the pole that sits on the standards to form a jump. It can also refer to the fence around the show ring.

Reserve Champion – is the person with the second highest amount of points in a division based on the ribbons awarded in the classes. This person receives a large ribbon that is made up of red, yellow and white ribbons.

Rollback – is a tight turn in a jumping course.

Rolltop – is a jump that looks like a rolltop desk. It is wider than a normal fence and solid.

Rotation – is a smaller group of riders in a jumping division. Each person in the rotation trades off trips in the ring until the group has ridden all the jumping classes in that division

Schooling – is considered a training ride during the show. These rides warm up the horse and the rider.

Schooling pads – are the larger, rectangular quilted pads. They provide better coverage on the horse and are used for lessons and schooling at shows.

Show pads – are saddle pads used for shows. They are white fleece, and extend outside around the saddle a couple of inches. They come in sizes geared to fit saddles of the same size. Look for pads that are fleece on top and quilted on the bottom. These hold their shape better than the all fleece version. Jumpers often use a fancier version of schooling pads in the show ring.

Simple lead change – refers to a lead change that is done as a series of steps. The horse goes from cantering to trotting, and then when the canter is picked back up, the horse is on the opposite lead.

Sitting trot – refers to the rider. When the horse is trotting, the rider is sitting rather than posting.

Standards – are the sides of the jumps on which the rails rest.

Stirrups – are attached to the saddle and are where riders put their feet while riding.

Stirrups (on jodhpurs) – are elastic bands that go over the rider's paddock boots and sit next to the heel of the boot.

Tall boots – extend up to the knee of the rider. They are black leather and can either pull on or zip up the back. It is becoming difficult to find pull-on boots, and zip-up boots are much easier to put on and take off. However, we had a zipper break at a show...not fun at all!

Trainer – is your child's coach and the person who trains your child's horse.

Trainer conflicts – occur when a trainer is coaching different riders in different classes at the same time. Unfortunately, he or she can only be in one place at a time. The trainer will work with the in-gate people at each ring to resolve these conflicts.

Trip – is a jumping round. These classes are often marked as O/F for over fences.

Under saddle – are classes that are judged on the horse. The rider's challenge is to make the horse look good.

7 Reference Guides

7.1 Car Loading Checklist

— Helmet
— Garment bag of show clothes
  o Show pants
  o Show jacket
  o Show shirt and collars (and pins)
  o Socks
  o Belt

— Hairnets, rubber bands, bobby pins, ribbons
— Boots
— Shoe shine kit
— Camera/video camera
— Cooler
— Chairs
— Bikes
— Clothes, toiletries (make sure you remember any prescription medication)

If not being shipped separately, or if you took them home to launder, don't forget:

— Saddle
— Saddle pads
— Girth

7.2 Tack Trunk Checklist

— Saddle (unless packed separately)
— Bridle and martingale
— Girth
— Crop and Spurs
— Half chaps for schooling
— Hoof dressing
— Fly spray
— Grooming brushes, tail brush, curry comb
— Towels
— Finishing spray/hair polish
— Shampoo
— Scraper
— Leg wraps
— Liniment and latex gloves
— Saddle soap/leather cleaner
— Sponges
— Tack box/show bag
— Show saddle pads and schooling pad
— Ear plugs
— Cooler blanket and Stable blanket
— Halter and Lead rope
— Buckets
— Jumping boots
— Lunge line
— Draw reins
— Hangers for buckets/halter, bridle
— Stall guard for hanging blankets
— Duct tape
— Scissors
— Pen
— Horse treats
— Safety pins, bobby pins, hairnets
— Moleskin, band aids
— Wet wipes

7.3   Show Ring Checklist

— Water
— Hoof dressing
— Fly spray
— Towel
— Collar & pin
— Show gloves
— Pen
— Tail brush
— Grooming brush
— Horse treats
— Snack
— Hoof pick
— Spray gel
— Scissors
— Safety pins
— Bobbie pins
— Spurs
— Crop
— Sunscreen
— Camera/video camera

7.4 Ribbons Awarded

Place	Color	Points toward Champion
1st	Blue	10
2nd	Red	6
3rd	Yellow	4
4th	White	2
5th	Pink	1
6th	Green	$\frac{1}{2}$

The champion of a division is determined by the highest number of total points based on the ribbons awarded for each class. The reserve champion is the person with the next highest amount of points. Ties are normally broken by reviewing who placed higher in the over fences (jumping) classes.

About the Author

Liz Page learned the workings of hunter jumper horse shows over many years of watching her daughter compete. Beginning with Walk-Trot and continuing through Jumper divisions, she slowly began to comprehend the confusing terms, strangely named divisions, and the important role parents play in supporting their children at shows. After wishing for a book that explained this bewildering world, she was inspired to write one herself when a fellow mom arrived at the barn with a pair of breeches instead of the jodhpurs she had been directed to buy.

Liz holds a doctorate degree in Atmospheric Science and develops distance learning courses for weather forecasters around the world. She recently relocated with her family and numerous animals to Colorado where she spends much of her spare time at the barn.

CPSIA information can be obtained
at www.ICGtesting.com
Printed in the USA
BVHW041833020921
615920BV00013B/490